How Hackers Can Crush You: Protecting Yourself and Keeping Your Kids and Family Safe Online

TABLE OF CONTENTS

Meet Craig Petronella..5
Chapter 1- What you need to know................................9
- Who and What is at Risk
- Initial Steps to keep your family safe

Chapter 2- Cyberbullying...14
- What is Cyberbullying and How do You Recognize it?
- Cyberbullying Example
- Real-Life Consequences of Cyberbullying
  - How to protect your family from cyberbullying

Chapter 3- Online Predators...21
- Who are Online Predators and how Do You Recognize Them?
- Online Predator Example
- Real-life consequences of Interaction with Online Predators
- How to protect your family from Online Predators

Chapter 4- Sextortion..29
- What Is Sextortion and how Do You Recognize It?
- Sextortion Example
- Real-life consequences of Sextortion
- How to protect your family from Sextortion

Chapter 5- Inappropriate Content................................34
- How to recognize inappropriate content
- Real Life Example

- Consequences of inappropriate content
- How to protect your family from inappropriate content

Chapter 6- Phishing and Scams……………………...............…..44
- How to recognize phishing and scams
- Real Life Example
- Consequences of Cyber Bullying
- How to protect your family from phishing and scams

Chapter 7- Overuse and Addiction……………………….52
- How to recognize overuse and addiction
- Real Life Example
- Consequences of overuse and addiction
- How to protect your family from overuse and addiction

Chapter 8- Privacy Concerns……………..………….……59
- How to recognize privacy concerns
- Real Life Example
- Consequences of privacy concerns
- How to protect your family from privacy concerns

Chapter 9- Cyber Security Threats…………….…..…….67
- How to recognize cybersecurity threats
- Real Life Example
- Consequences of cybersecurity threats
- How to Protect your family from cybersecurity threats

Chapter 10- Social Media……………….…………….……66
- Importance and potential risks
- Setting and keeping boundaries
- Staying vigilant

Chapter 11- Nightmare IRL:Discord and Telegram.82

Chapter 12- Keeping Your Family Safe……………..…..86
- Practical Steps
- Timeline

Chapter 13- Tools of the Trade…………….…………….101
- Recommended software
- How these tools keep your family safe
- How to keep these tools up to date

Chapter 14- Teach Them Early…………………….……..104
- 10 Steps to Educate Cyber Savvy Kids
- Clear and consistent Communication

Chapter 15- Issues on the Horizon……………………….109
- AI
- IoT Devices

- VR and AR
- Esports
- Deepfakes and Misinformation
- Biometric and Facial Recognition

Chapter 16- Staying Ahead of the Threat……………......…112
- Education
- Boundaries
- Security Protocols for the whole family
- Vigilance

Meet Craig Petronella

Craig Petronella, IT Cybersecurity and Compliance Expert and Petronella Technology Group, Inc.

*Craig Petronella, CMMC-RP
IT Cybersecurity and
Compliance Expert*

- Amazon #1 Best-Selling Author of many books, including "The Ultimate Guide To CMMC", How HIPAA Can Crush Your Medical Practice and more.
- Licensed Digital Forensics Examiner (DFE)
- CMMC certified registered practitioner (RP)
- Contributing Editor of Triangle Attorney Magazine
- Expert Testimony

- Platinum Certified Constant Contact (Formerly Sharpspring) Marketing Automation Expert
- DigitalMarketer Digital Marketing Expert
- Cisco Certified CCNA
- Hubbell Certified
- Proxim Certified CWNE
- Over 30 years of experience helping federal contractors and businesses with cybersecurity, digital forensics and compliance regulations.
- Certified through MIT, IBM, Cisco, and other major channels in Artificial Intelligence (AI), Blockchain, CMMC, HIPAA, Cybersecurity and Compliance.
- Founded Petronella Technology Group, Inc. (PTG) dba Petronella Cybersecurity and Digital Forensics in April of 2002. PTG is a registered provider organization (RPO) with the Cyberab.org that provides US-based consulting, managed services, co-managed IT, and managed cybersecurity services to customers across many verticals in both public and private organizations. We understand that every industry and organization can be faced with unique IT challenges. Our expertise enables us to help clients navigate the requirements of their industry – such as CJIS for state and local governments, CMMC for organizations working with controlled unclassified information (CUI), NIST 800-171 and DFARS for defense industrial base contractors, HIPAA, HITECH, PCI-DSS and more. Founded https://ComplianceArmor.com, a division of PTG specializing in training, automation, policies, and procedures in 2016. Founded https://BlockchainSecurity.com, a division of PTG specializing in Blockchain and Crypto in 2017. Founded https://simplecyber.io/ in 2024 offering fully AI-based IT & Cyber.
- Host of the podcast called Cybersecurity and Compliance with Craig Petronella - CMMC, NIST, DFARS, HIPAA, GDPR, ISO27001 https://petronellatech.com/podcasts/

Craig Petronella frequently assists law enforcement and attorneys with various cases involving cybercrime including but not limited to: Business Email Compromise (BEC), ransomware investigations, data breaches, cryptocurrency tracing, investigations and more.

Petronella's Certified CMMC Registered Practitioners (RPs) are fully background checked and will leverage our industry experience to partner with you to help you comply with CMMC and other regulations. This includes readiness consulting, security risk assessments, tabletop exercises, penetration testing, training, security controls, design, implementation, and ongoing managed security services.

Petronella® gets your business secure and compliant by doing 80% of the cybersecurity and compliance work for you by leveraging our proven ComplianceArmor.com® IP, policies, procedures and secure, custom, private-cloud, hosting services that protect your business with a unique, proven, patented, 39+ layer cybersecurity stack that is often faster, more secure and affordable than comparable FedRamp hosting!

Call 919-422-2607 or Schedule a Call with Craig Petronella Today using the link: https://go.oncehub.com/cmmc

As Seen on ABC, CBS, NBC, FOX, NewsObserver.com and more!

CHAPTER 1

What You Need to Know

Who and What is at Risk

If you picked up a copy of this book, you know just how important it is to keep your family safe from hackers. While an incredible tool for learning and connecting, the internet poses significant dangers for kids and families. The vast amount of easily accessible information means children can stumble upon inappropriate content such as violence, pornography, or hate speech, which can have long-lasting psychological effects.

Online predators often lurk in chat rooms, social media platforms, and gaming sites, posing as peers to manipulate and exploit children. This danger is exacerbated by the internet's anonymity, making it difficult for parents to monitor their children's interactions effectively.

The internet can foster addictive behaviors, especially in children who are still developing self-regulation skills. Social media platforms, online gaming, and streaming services offer endless entertainment and instant gratification, leading to excessive screen time and neglect of real-life responsibilities. This addiction not only affects academic performance and physical health but also strains family relationships as children become increasingly isolated and withdrawn.

The internet presents privacy and security risks for families. Children may inadvertently share personal information online, making them vulnerable to identity theft, cyberbullying, or even physical harm. The prevalence of scams and malware poses a threat to the financial security of families, with cybercriminals targeting unsuspecting users through phishing emails, fake websites, and malicious software. So, while the internet offers numerous benefits, parents must educate themselves and their children about online safety measures to mitigate these risks effectively.

Cybersecurity breaches pose significant dangers for families, jeopardizing their privacy, finances, and even physical safety.

A breach in cybersecurity can result in the unauthorized access of sensitive personal information, including financial records, medical history, and contact details. This information can be exploited by cybercriminals for identity theft, fraud, or harassment, leading to severe financial and emotional consequences for the affected family members.

Additionally, the increasing connectivity of household devices through the Internet of Things (IoT), such as smart TVs, thermostats, and security cameras, a breach in cybersecurity could compromise the safety and security of the entire household.

Cybersecurity breaches can have profound financial implications for families. Cybercriminals may gain access to banking or credit card information, draining accounts or making unauthorized purchases. Additionally, ransomware attacks can encrypt valuable data on family computers or devices, demanding payment for its release. The financial strain resulting from these breaches can be significant, affecting the family's ability to meet basic needs and causing long-term financial instability.

Finally, cybersecurity breaches can disrupt the normal functioning of family life, causing stress and anxiety. Family members may feel violated and vulnerable knowing that their personal information has been compromised. The time and resources required to recover from a cybersecurity breach, including securing accounts, repairing devices, and seeking legal assistance, can strain family relationships and detract from quality time spent together. Because of the cyber world we all live in, families need to prioritize cybersecurity measures, to safeguard against these potential dangers now more than ever.

Initial Steps to Keep Your Family Safe

The online landscape poses various risks to children and teens, and parents should be vigilant in safeguarding them against these threats. Devices should be up to date with the latest operating system software (OS) as well as the latest security patches. If the device is old or outdated and cannot be patched, it should not be used online as it poses a major security threat!

Every piece of software and/or "app" (application) that is downloaded also needs to be vetted, tested, and updated. Make sure to only install the necessary software to fit your family's needs. Free software can be appealing to families trying to save on expensive name-brand software. However, free software is particularly risky because rogue developers will embed spyware or other types of surveillance software in the background, silently exfiltrating information without your knowledge. Make sure to do your research on the developers and the country of origin of all software and apps used in your household. Apple and Google Play stores have let thousands of infected apps into their stores!

Keeping kids safe online requires a multi-faceted approach that involves education, communication, and constant monitoring. Parents should educate their children about the potential dangers of the internet, including cyberbullying, online predators, and exposure to inappropriate content. This education should start at an early age and include open and honest discussions about safe online behavior. As parents, it is your job to set clear rules and boundaries for internet use, establish guidelines for which websites and apps are appropriate, and enforce time limits for screen time.

Open communication between parents and children is crucial for keeping kids safe online. Parents should encourage their children to feel comfortable discussing their online experiences and concerns openly. By fostering a non-judgmental and supportive environment, parents can build trust with their children and empower them to seek help if they encounter anything distressing online. Regular check-ins about online activities, interests, and friendships can help parents stay informed about their children's online behavior and address any potential issues proactively.

Parents should utilize parental control tools and monitoring software to help manage and supervise their children's online activities. These tools can enable parents to filter or block inappropriate content, set age-appropriate restrictions on websites and apps, and monitor their children's internet usage and social media interactions. This book will take a deep dive into these tactics, tools, and practices for your whole family.

CHAPTER 2

Cyber Bullying

What is Cyberbullying and How Do You Recognize It?

Cyberbullying refers to the use of digital technologies, such as social media, text messages, or online platforms, to harass, intimidate, or harm others. It involves repetitive and intentional actions to cause emotional distress, humiliation, or fear in the victim. Cyberbullying can take various forms, including spreading rumors, sharing embarrassing or private information, creating fake profiles, sending threatening messages, or excluding someone from online groups.

Recognizing cyberbullying is crucial for addressing and preventing its harmful effects. Signs that someone may be a victim of cyberbullying include sudden changes in behavior, reluctance to use or withdraw from electronic devices, avoidance of social activities, declining academic performance, or expressing fear or anxiety about going online. Additionally, if a child becomes upset, angry, or secretive while using digital devices, it could be indicative of cyberbullying.

On the other hand, recognizing the behavior of a cyberbully is equally important. A cyberbully may exhibit aggression, impulsivity, and a desire for power and control. They may create and share hurtful content, engage in online arguments, or demonstrate a pattern of targeting specific individuals. Monitoring a child's online activities and maintaining open communication can help parents and guardians recognize signs of cyberbullying early on.

To address cyberbullying, parents, educators, and peers need to promote a culture of digital responsibility. Encouraging open communication with children about their online experiences, fostering empathy, and educating them about appropriate online behavior can contribute to creating a safer online environment. If cyberbullying is suspected, it's important to report incidents to relevant authorities, schools, or social media platforms and work collaboratively to provide support for the victim and consequences for the perpetrator. This reporting has quite literally saved lives.

Cyberbullying Example

Let's consider a hypothetical example of cyberbullying involving two high school students, Alex and Emily. Alex, feeling jealous of Emily's popularity, creates a fake Instagram account under a pseudonym and starts posting hurtful comments about Emily's appearance and social status. These comments quickly escalate into derogatory messages and rumors, causing Emily significant distress. Despite her attempts to ignore the harassment, the hurtful messages continue to spread, and Emily's self-esteem begins to plummet.

Recognizing the signs of distress in Emily, her close friend notices her sudden withdrawal from social activities and changes in behavior. Concerned, the friend initiates a conversation with Emily, who reluctantly confides in her about cyberbullying. With Emily's permission, the friend alerts their school counselor and provides evidence of the online harassment. The counselor takes immediate action, involving school administrators and Emily's parents in the situation.

Meanwhile, Alex's behavior is also brought to the attention of his parents when they notice him spending an excessive amount of time on his phone and exhibiting signs of agitation. After a heart-to-heart conversation with his parents, Alex admits to his involvement in cyberbullying and expresses remorse for his actions. Recognizing the seriousness of the situation, Alex's parents work with the school and Emily's family to address the harm caused and provide support for both Emily and Alex.

As a resolution, Alex is required to apologize to Emily in person, delete the fake Instagram account, and attend counseling sessions to address the underlying issues contributing to his behavior. Additionally, the school implements educational programs on cyberbullying awareness and digital citizenship to prevent similar incidents in the future. Through collaborative efforts between the school, parents, and students, the situation is resolved, and both Emily and Alex receive the support they need to heal from the cyberbullying incident.

Even this is a tame example. As our family's guardians, we must know how to prevent a situation like this.

Real-Life Consequences of Cyberbullying

Cyberbullying can have devastating real-life consequences for both the victims and the perpetrators involved. For victims, the psychological impact of cyberbullying can be profound, leading to increased levels of stress, anxiety, depression, and low self-esteem. Victims may experience feelings of isolation, shame, and fear, which can affect their ability to concentrate in school, maintain healthy relationships, and engage in social activities. In severe cases, cyberbullying has been linked to suicidal ideation and attempts, highlighting the seriousness of its effects on mental health.

Cyberbullying can have lasting repercussions on victims' academic and professional lives. Persistent harassment and humiliation online can lead to declines in academic performance, absenteeism from school, and even dropping out altogether.

Additionally, the spread of false rumors or damaging content online can tarnish a victim's reputation and hinder their future opportunities for employment or higher education. The digital nature of cyberbullying means that harmful content can spread rapidly and persist indefinitely, making it challenging for victims to escape the consequences.

For perpetrators of cyberbullying, there are also significant real-life consequences. In addition to potential legal repercussions, such as charges of harassment or defamation, perpetrators may face disciplinary actions from schools, including suspension or expulsion. Engaging in cyberbullying behavior can have long-term effects on the perpetrator's own mental health and social relationships. Feelings of guilt, remorse, and shame may arise because of their actions, leading to social ostracism and strained relationships with family and peers. Additionally, involvement in cyberbullying can hinder the perpetrator's personal and professional development, as it may signal a lack of empathy, impulse control, and conflict resolution skills.

The real-life consequences of cyberbullying underscore the need for proactive measures to prevent and address this harmful behavior effectively.

How to protect your family from cyberbullying

Parents can help by encouraging open communication with their children, teaching them how to block and report bullies, and monitoring their online activities for signs of bullying. If possible, try to avoid social media altogether. There is new research showing the harmful effects of social media as well as new legislation in the works that may restrict certain ages from using social media. Try to only allow what is necessary. Consider a locked-down mobile device such as a Gabb Watch or Gabb Phone where there is no internet or social media. Only approved apps from Gabb are permitted.

Below are 7 steps you and your family can also take to ensure that you are protected from cyberbullying.

1. **Educate your family:** Teach your children about the dangers of cyberbullying, including how to recognize it and what steps to take if they experience or witness it. Discuss appropriate online behavior, empathy, and respect for others.

2. **Establish clear guidelines:** Set rules for internet and device usage within your family, including guidelines for what websites and apps are allowed, how much time can be spent online, and when devices should be turned off. Reinforce the importance of privacy and responsible digital citizenship.

3. **Encourage open communication:** Create a safe and supportive environment where your children feel comfortable discussing their online experiences and concerns. Regularly check in with them about their online activities and friendships and listen to any issues they may encounter without judgment.

4. **Monitor online activity:** Keep an eye on your children's online interactions by monitoring their browsing history, social media accounts, and messages. Use parental control software or privacy settings to restrict access to inappropriate content and monitor their online behavior for signs of cyberbullying.

5. **Teach resilience:** Help your children develop resilience and coping strategies to deal with cyberbullying. Encourage them to block or unfriend cyberbullies, report abusive behavior to the appropriate authorities or platforms and seek

support from trusted adults, friends, or helplines if needed.

6. **Lead by example:** Set a positive example for your children by modeling respectful and responsible online behavior yourself. Avoid engaging in cyberbullying or sharing hurtful content and demonstrate empathy and kindness towards others online.

7. **Stay informed:** Stay up to date on the latest trends and technologies related to cyberbullying and educate yourself about the warning signs and potential risks. Be proactive in addressing any issues that arise and seek support from schools, counselors, or online safety organizations if needed.

By taking proactive steps to educate, communicate, and monitor your family's online activities, you can help protect them from the harmful effects of cyberbullying and create a safer digital environment for everyone.

CHAPTER 3

Online Predators

<u>Who are Online Predators and how Do You Recognize Them?</u>

Online predators are individuals who use the internet to exploit and manipulate others, typically targeting children and adolescents for grooming, manipulation, and exploitation. These predators often pose as peers, authority figures, or trusted individuals to gain the trust of their victims and manipulate them into engaging in inappropriate or harmful activities.

Recognizing online predators can be challenging, as they often use deception and manipulation to disguise their true intentions. However, there are some common warning signs to look out for:

1. **Overly friendly or secretive behavior:** Online predators may initially be very friendly and supportive towards their victims, showering them with attention, compliments, and gifts. They may also encourage secrecy and discourage their victims from sharing information about their online interactions with others.

2. **Attempts to establish trust:** Predators may try to gain the trust of their victims by pretending to

have similar interests, experiences, or backgrounds. They may also use flattery or manipulation to build emotional connections with their victims and lower their defenses.

3. **Requests for personal information:** Predators may ask their victims for personal information such as their age, location, school, or contact details. They may use this information to gather more information about their victims or to manipulate them into meeting in person.

4. **Attempts to isolate victims:** Predators may try to isolate their victims from their friends and family by encouraging them to spend more time online or by discouraging them from participating in offline activities. They may also try to alienate their victims from their support networks by spreading rumors or lies.

5. **Pressure for sexual activity:** In cases of sexual exploitation, predators may try to pressure their victims into engaging in sexual activities or sending explicit images or videos. They may use threats, coercion, or manipulation to intimidate their victims into complying with their demands.

6. **Inconsistencies in their story:** Online predators may provide inconsistent or contradictory information about themselves, their intentions, or their background. They may also avoid answering questions or provide vague or evasive responses when asked direct questions.

It's important for parents and guardians to stay vigilant and monitor their children's online activities, as well as educate them about the risks of interacting with strangers online. Encourage open communication with your children and teach them about appropriate online behavior, boundaries, and how to recognize and respond to potential threats from online predators. If you suspect that an online predator is targeting your child, take immediate action to protect them and report the incident to the authorities.

Online Predator Example

In this hypothetical scenario, let's consider a situation involving a teenage boy named Jake and an online predator named Taylor. Jake, a 15-year-old, is an avid gamer who enjoys connecting with others online through a popular gaming platform. One day, he receives a private message from Taylor, who claims to be a fellow gamer around the same age. Taylor seems friendly and shares common interests with Jake, initiating conversations about their favorite games and strategies.

As the online friendship progresses, Taylor begins to ask Jake personal questions, such as his location, school, and daily routine. Taylor claims to be from a nearby town and suggests they meet up to play games together in person. Despite feeling a bit uneasy about sharing personal information and meeting in real life, Jake hesitates to reject Taylor, fearing he might lose a gaming companion and want to be perceived as friendly.

Recognizing the potential danger, Jake's older sibling, Emily, becomes suspicious of the situation. Emily, who is aware of the risks associated with online interactions, decides to talk to Jake about his conversations with Taylor. Emily educates Jake about the dangers of sharing personal information online and the importance of setting boundaries with strangers. She encourages Jake to cease communication with Taylor immediately and report the user to the gaming platform's moderation team.

Together, Jake and Emily report Taylor's suspicious behavior to the gaming platform, providing screenshots of the concerning messages. The platform takes swift action, investigating the reported user and finding evidence of predatory behavior.

They promptly suspended Taylor's account and notified law enforcement about the potential threat.

Simultaneously, Emily and Jake's parents involve local authorities, who conduct a thorough investigation to ensure Jake's safety. With the cooperation of the gaming platform and the prompt intervention of Jake's family, Taylor is identified and apprehended, facing legal consequences for attempted child exploitation.

In this resolved scenario, the combination of awareness, communication, and proactive reporting contributes to the protection of Jake and the prevention of further harm. The incident emphasizes the importance of fostering open communication within families about online safety and promptly addressing any signs of potential danger.

Real-life Consequences of Interaction with Online Predators

The consequences of interacting with online predators can be severe and have long-lasting impacts on the victims' physical, emotional, and psychological well-being. Here are some potential consequences:

1. **Emotional and Psychological Trauma:** Victims of online predators may experience intense feelings of fear, shame, guilt, and betrayal. They may suffer from anxiety, depression, and post-traumatic stress disorder (PTSD) as a result of the exploitation and manipulation they endured. The emotional trauma inflicted by online predators can have long-lasting effects on victims' mental health and well-being.

2. **Physical Harm:** In cases where online predators successfully lure their victims into meeting in person, there is a risk of physical harm or assault. Victims may be subjected to abduction, sexual assault, or violence, putting their safety and physical

integrity at serious risk. Even if no physical harm occurs, the fear and trauma associated with the encounter can be deeply damaging.

3. **Social and Behavioral Consequences:** Interactions with online predators can have social and behavioral consequences for victims, affecting their relationships, academic performance, and functioning. Victims may withdraw from social activities, experience difficulties trusting others, and struggle with feelings of isolation and alienation. They may also exhibit changes in behavior, such as aggression, self-harm, or substance abuse, as a way of coping with their trauma.

4. **Cybersecurity Risks:** Victims of online predators may also face cybersecurity risks, such as identity theft, financial fraud, or exposure of personal information. Predators may use the information they gather during online interactions to exploit their victims further or to target them for cyberattacks. This can have serious implications for victims' privacy, security, and financial stability.

How to protect your family from Online Predators

Protecting your family from online predators requires a proactive approach that combines education, communication, and vigilant monitoring. Here are some steps you can take:

1. **Educate your family:** Teach your children about the dangers of online predators, including how they operate and the tactics they use to manipulate and exploit their victims. Help them understand the importance of privacy, setting boundaries, and being cautious when interacting with strangers online.

2. **Encourage open communication:** Create a safe and

supportive environment where your children feel comfortable discussing their online experiences and concerns. Encourage them to come to you if they encounter anything suspicious or uncomfortable online and reassure them that they won't get in trouble for seeking help.

3. **Set clear boundaries:** Establish rules and guidelines for internet and device usage within your family, including what websites and apps are allowed, how much time can be spent online, and when devices should be turned off. Monitor your children's online activities and enforce consequences for violating family rules.

4. **Monitor online activity:** Keep an eye on your children's online interactions by monitoring their browsing history, social media accounts, and messaging apps. Use parental control software or privacy settings to restrict access to inappropriate content and monitor their online behavior for signs of grooming or manipulation by predators.

5. **Teach critical thinking skills:** Help your children develop critical thinking skills to evaluate online content and recognize potential threats from online predators. Teach them to question the authenticity of strangers online, verify information before sharing personal details, and trust their instincts if something feels off.

6. **Model healthy online behavior:** Set a positive example for your children by modeling responsible and respectful online behavior yourself. Avoid sharing personal information or engaging in risky behaviors online and demonstrate empathy and kindness towards others in your online interactions.

7. **Stay informed and engaged:** Stay up to date on the latest trends and technologies related to online safety and cyber threats. Engage with your children about their online activities regularly, asking questions and showing genuine interest in their online experiences.

By taking proactive steps to educate, communicate, and monitor your family's online activities, you can help protect them from online predators and create a safer digital environment for everyone.

CHAPTER 4

Sextortion

What Is Sextortion and how Do You Recognize It?

Sextortion is a form of blackmail where someone coerces children, teens and other family members into providing sexual images, videos, or performing sexual acts, usually over the internet. Recognizing sextortion involves staying cautious of requests for explicit content, threats to share private photos or videos, and demands for money or further sexual acts in exchange for not sharing the content. It's important to trust your instincts, not share compromising material with strangers, and seek help from authorities or support services if you feel targeted or threatened.

By the Numbers[1]
In 2023, the CyberTipline received **186,819** reports of online enticement, the category that includes sextortion.

Between 2021 and 2023, the number of online enticement reports increased by **323%**

Sextortion Example

An example of sextortion could involve someone pretending to be a romantic interest or acquaintance online, gaining the trust of the victim, and convincing them to send explicit photos or videos. Once the perpetrator has these materials, they threaten to share them publicly unless the victim provides more explicit content or money. This manipulation preys on the victim's fear and vulnerability, leading them to comply with the demands out of fear of humiliation or other consequences. Being aware of such tactics and reporting any suspicious behavior can help prevent falling victim to sextortion.

Real-life consequences of Sextortion

The consequences of sextortion can have devastating impacts on individuals' lives. Some real-life consequences include:

1. Emotional trauma and distress: Victims of sextortion often experience high levels of shame, embarrassment, anxiety, and depression due to the violation of their privacy and the fear of exposure.

2. Damage to reputation: If explicit images or videos are shared publicly, victims may face humiliation, social stigma, and damage to their personal and professional reputation.

3. Financial loss: Perpetrators of sextortion may demand money from victims in exchange for not sharing explicit content. Victims who comply with these demands may suffer financial loss.

4. Legal repercussions: In some cases, sextortion can lead to legal consequences for both the victim and the perpetrator, such as charges related to extortion, harassment, or distribution of child pornography.

5. Relationship strains: Sextortion incidents can strain relationships with family, friends, and partners due

to the sensitive nature of the situation and the potential breach of trust.

It is crucial to seek support, report the incident to authorities, and access resources for help if you or someone you know has experienced sextortion.

How to protect your family from Sextortion

Protecting your family from sextortion involves a combination of awareness, communication, and proactive measures. Here are some steps you can take:

1. Educate Your Family: Teach your family members, especially children and teenagers, about the risks associated with sharing sensitive information online. Explain what sextortion is and how it can happen.

2. Privacy Settings: Ensure that privacy settings are configured correctly on social media accounts and other online platforms. Limit who can see personal information and posts.

3. Strong Passwords: Encourage the use of strong, unique passwords for each online account. Consider using a password manager to generate and store passwords securely.

4. Think Before Sharing: Emphasize the importance of thinking before sharing anything online, especially photos or videos that could be used for blackmail.

5. Keep Personal Information Private: Advise your family members not to share personal information such as addresses, phone numbers, or financial details with strangers online.

6. Verify Contacts: Teach your family members to verify the identity of individuals they communicate with online before sharing personal information or engaging in sensitive conversations.

7. Monitor Online Activity: Keep an eye on your family's online activity, especially for younger members. Establish open communication so they feel comfortable discussing any concerns or suspicious interactions.

8. Report Suspicious Activity: Encourage your family members to report any suspicious messages or interactions to the appropriate authorities, such as the police or internet service providers.

9. Stay Updated on Scams*: Stay informed about the latest scams and techniques used by perpetrators of sextortion. This knowledge can help you recognize and avoid potential threats.

10. Seek Support: If someone in your family becomes a victim of sextortion, offer them emotional support and encourage them to seek help from law enforcement and other support services.

11. Visit TakeItDown.mcnec.org to begin the process of having any unwanted illicit photos taken off the internet.

By taking these proactive steps, you can help protect your family from falling victim to sextortion and empower them to stay safe online.

CHAPTER 5

Inappropriate Content

What is Inappropriate Content and How Do You Recognize it?

Inappropriate content for kids online can vary widely, but generally includes material that is not suitable for children due to its explicit, violent, or otherwise harmful nature. Here are some common types of inappropriate content for kids online and how you can recognize them:

1. **Violent or Graphic Content**: This includes depictions of violence, gore, or other graphic imagery. It may be found in video games, videos, or images. Signs of violent or graphic content include realistic depictions of blood, injuries, or intense combat scenes.

2. **Sexually Explicit Material**: Content that is sexually explicit or pornographic is highly inappropriate for children. Signs of such content include nudity, sexual acts, or sexually suggestive language or imagery.

3. **Hate Speech or Discrimination**: Material that promotes hate speech, discrimination, or prejudice against individuals or groups based on factors such as race, ethnicity, religion, gender, sexual orientation, or disability is harmful for children. Look out

for derogatory language, stereotypes, or messages promoting intolerance.

4. **Drug and Alcohol Use**: Content that glamorizes or promotes substance abuse, including drugs and alcohol, is not suitable for children. This may include images, videos, or discussions about drug use, alcohol consumption, or addiction.

5. **Cyberbullying**: Content that involves harassment, bullying, or intimidation of individuals online can be harmful to children's mental and emotional well-being. Signs of cyberbullying include mean or threatening messages, exclusion, or spreading rumors.

6. **Unsafe or Dangerous Activities**: Material that encourages or depicts unsafe or dangerous behaviors, such as self-harm, suicide, or risky stunts, can pose serious risks to children. Look for content that glorifies dangerous activities or provides instructions for harmful behaviors.

7. **Inappropriate Language**: Content containing strong language, vulgarities, or explicit references to bodily functions or anatomy may not be suitable for children.

To recognize inappropriate content for kids online, parents and caregivers can:

- Monitor children's online activities and supervise their internet usage.
- Use parental control tools and filters to block or restrict access to inappropriate content.
- Educate children about safe and responsible internet usage, including how to recognize and avoid inappropriate content.

- Encourage open communication with children so they feel comfortable discussing any concerns or questions about the content they encounter online.
- Stay informed about popular websites, apps, and online trends, and be vigilant for any signs of inappropriate content.

Inappropriate Content Example

Kids can stumble across inappropriate content online through various avenues, often unintentionally. Here are some common ways this might happen:

1. **Unfiltered Internet Access**: Children may come across inappropriate content while browsing the internet without proper supervision or controls in place. Without parental controls or filters, they can easily stumble upon inappropriate websites, images, or videos.

2. **Search Engine Results**: Even innocuous search queries can sometimes yield results that include inappropriate content. Children might inadvertently click on links that lead them to sites containing explicit material or other inappropriate content.

3. **Pop-Up Ads**: Pop-up ads can appear on websites, even those that are generally considered safe for children. These ads may contain inappropriate content or links to sites with such material, and children may click on them out of curiosity.

4. **Social Media**: Children may encounter inappropriate content on social media platforms, either through their own exploration or by viewing content shared by their peers or followers. This can include images, videos, or posts containing violence, explicit language, or other inappropriate material.

5. **Online Gaming Communities**: Some online gaming communities may contain inappropriate content, such as chat messages or user-generated content that is not moderated effectively. Children who participate in these communities may inadvertently come across inappropriate language, discussions, or imagery.

6. **Links Shared by Friends or Peers**: Kids may receive links to websites, videos, or other online content from their friends or peers, without realizing that the content is inappropriate. This can happen through messaging apps, email, social media, or other forms of communication.

7. **Misleading or Deceptive Content**: Sometimes, content may be misleadingly labeled or disguised to appear harmless or appropriate for children when it is actually inappropriate. Children may click on such content without realizing the nature of what they are accessing.

8. **Online Challenges or Trends**: Certain online challenges, trends, or viral content may involve or depict inappropriate behavior. Children may come across such content while browsing or participating in online communities or platforms.

To mitigate the risk of children stumbling across inappropriate content online, it's important for parents and caregivers to actively monitor and supervise their internet usage, set up parental controls and filters, educate children about safe online behavior, and maintain open communication about what they encounter online.

<u>Real-life Consequences of Interaction with Inappropriate Content</u>

Interacting with inappropriate content online can have various real-life consequences for children, including:

1. **Emotional and Psychological Effects**: Exposure to violent, sexual, or otherwise disturbing content can lead to feelings of fear, anxiety, confusion, or distress in children. Such experiences may have long-lasting effects on their mental and emotional well-being, potentially leading to trauma or other psychological issues.

2. **Desensitization**: Repeated exposure to inappropriate content can desensitize children to violence, sexual imagery, or other harmful behaviors. This desensitization may lead them to perceive such content as normal or acceptable, potentially influencing their attitudes and behaviors offline.

3. **Behavioral Changes**: Interacting with inappropriate content may influence children's behavior, leading to aggression, acting out, or imitating harmful actions they have seen online. They may also exhibit changes in mood, social interactions, or academic performance as a result of their exposure to such content.

4. **Developmental Impact**: Inappropriate content can interfere with children's cognitive and emotional development by exposing them to concepts or experiences they are not equipped to understand or process. This can hinder their ability to form healthy relationships, regulate their emotions, or develop critical thinking skills.

5. **Safety Risks**: Some inappropriate content may encourage or glorify risky or dangerous behaviors, such as substance abuse, self-harm, or participation in unsafe challenges or stunts. Children who emulate these behaviors based on what they see online may put themselves at risk of physical harm or injury.

6. **Social and Peer Dynamics**: Interacting with inappropriate content online can impact children's relationships with their peers and their social dynamics. They may be influenced by peer pressure to engage with such content or feel isolated or ostracized if they choose not to participate.

7. **Legal Consequences**: In some cases, interacting with inappropriate content online may have legal ramifications, especially if it involves accessing or sharing illegal material such as child pornography, hate speech, or copyrighted material. Children who engage in such activities may face legal consequences or sanctions.

8. **Family and Parental Concerns**: Interactions with inappropriate content can cause tension within families and strain parent-child relationships. Parents may feel distressed or overwhelmed by their children's exposure to harmful content and may struggle to address the situation effectively.

The real-life consequences of interacting with inappropriate content online underscore the importance of parental supervision, education about safe internet usage, and fostering open communication between children and their caregivers about their online experiences. By taking proactive steps to protect children from harmful content and providing support and guidance when needed, adults can help mitigate the potential negative effects of online interactions.

How to protect your family from Inappropriate Content

Protecting your family from inappropriate content online requires a combination of strategies to minimize exposure and promote safe internet usage. Here are some steps you can take:

1. **Set Up Parental Controls**: Most devices, operating

systems, and internet service providers offer parental control features that allow you to restrict access to certain websites, apps, and content types. Take advantage of these controls to filter out inappropriate material and set time limits for internet usage.

2. **Use Safe Search Settings**: Enable safe search settings on search engines to filter out explicit or inappropriate content from search results. This can help prevent children from stumbling upon inappropriate material while conducting online searches.

3. **Install Content Filtering Software**: Consider installing content filtering software or parental control apps on your devices to block access to websites or apps that contain inappropriate content. These tools can also provide activity reports and alerts to help you monitor your family's online activities.

4. **Educate Your Family**: Teach your children about safe internet usage, including the importance of avoiding inappropriate content and interacting responsibly online. Discuss the potential risks and consequences of accessing or sharing inappropriate material and encourage them to come to you with any questions or concerns.

5. **Establish Clear Rules and Boundaries**: Establish rules and guidelines for internet usage within your family, including which websites and apps are off-limits and appropriate time limits for screen time. Enforce these rules consistently and discuss the reasons behind them with your children.

6. **Monitor Online Activities**: Regularly monitor your family's online activities, including the websites they

visit, the apps they use, and their social media interactions. Keep an eye out for any signs of inappropriate content or online behaviors that may indicate potential risks.

7. **Encourage Open Communication**: Foster open communication with your family about their online experiences and any concerns they may have encountered. Create a safe and supportive environment where your children feel comfortable discussing their online activities and seeking guidance when needed.

8. **Lead by Example**: Be a positive role model for your family by demonstrating responsible online behavior and setting a good example for how to interact safely and respectfully on the internet. Limit your own exposure to inappropriate content and prioritize quality time offline with your family.

9. **Stay Informed and Stay Engaged**: Keep yourself informed about the latest online trends, apps, and risks, and stay engaged in your family's online activities. Stay up to date on the content your children are consuming and be proactive in addressing any concerns that arise.

By implementing these strategies and actively monitoring your family's online activities, you can help protect them from inappropriate content and promote a safer and healthier online environment for everyone.

CHAPTER 6

Phishing and Scams

How to Recognize Phishing and Scams

R ecognizing phishing attempts and scams is essential in safeguarding oneself from online threats. One of the primary indicators of a phishing email is the sender's address. Pay close attention to any discrepancies or irregularities in the email address, such as misspellings or suspicious domain names that may differ from the legitimate organization's domain.

Scrutinize the email for urgent or alarming language designed to incite panic, as phishing emails often employ tactics to pressure recipients into taking immediate action, such as claiming that their account has been compromised or that they need to update their information urgently.

Another key aspect to look at is the authenticity of links embedded within the email. Hovering over links without clicking on them can reveal the actual URL destination, enabling you to detect any inconsistencies between the displayed link and the claimed destination. Phishing emails often lead to fraudulent websites that mimic legitimate ones in an attempt to trick users into providing sensitive information.

Be wary of emails containing spelling and grammar errors or unprofessional language, as these can indicate a lack of legitimacy. Legitimate organizations typically maintain a level of professionalism in their communication, and any deviations may suggest a phishing attempt.

Exercise caution when providing personal or financial information in response to unsolicited emails or messages. Legitimate organizations rarely request sensitive information via email, especially without prior contact or verification. When in doubt, verify the authenticity of the sender through official channels, such as contacting the organization directly or visiting their official website. By remaining vigilant, scrutinizing incoming communications, and staying informed about common phishing techniques, individuals can enhance their ability to recognize and avoid falling victim to phishing and scams.

Phishing and Scams Example

In a real-life example, let's consider a scenario where a group of teenagers falls victim to a phishing scam through a popular social media platform.

A cybercriminal creates a fake account impersonating a well-known celebrity or influencer, offering exclusive access to behind-the-scenes content, merchandise giveaways, or promises of fame and recognition. The fake account appears convincing, with a profile picture and username resembling the legitimate celebrity's account, making it difficult for the teens to discern the difference.

Enticed by the prospect of interacting with their favorite celebrity or gaining access to exclusive perks, the teenagers eagerly engage with the fake account, clicking on links provided in the messages or providing personal information when prompted. Unbeknownst to them, these actions lead to a phishing website designed to harvest their login credentials, credit card information, or other sensitive data. The phishing website may mimic the appearance of the legitimate social media platform or use other deceptive tactics to appear genuine.

As the teens continue to interact with the fake account, they may unknowingly share the phishing links with their friends, amplifying the scam's reach and causing further harm. Some may even fall victim to additional scams, such as identity theft or financial fraud, as their personal information is compromised. By the time they realize they've been duped, it may be too late to mitigate the damage, and they may face consequences such as unauthorized charges on their accounts or compromised online identities.

This example underscores the importance of educating children and teens about the dangers of phishing and scams, teaching them how to recognize suspicious messages and requests, and fostering open communication about their online activities. By empowering them with the knowledge and tools to protect themselves from online threats, parents and caregivers can help mitigate the risks of falling victim to phishing and scams in today's digital world.

Real-life Consequences of Phishing and Scams

Real-life consequences of falling victim to phishing and scams can be devastating, impacting victims both financially and emotionally. One significant consequence is financial loss. Scammers often deceive individuals into providing sensitive information such as bank account details, credit card numbers, or login credentials under false pretenses. Once obtained, this information can be used to make unauthorized purchases, drain bank accounts, or commit identity theft, leaving victims facing substantial financial hardships and the arduous task of recovering their stolen funds.

Phishing and scams can result in compromised personal information and identities. When victims unwittingly divulge sensitive data to cybercriminals, they put themselves at risk of identity theft and fraud. Stolen personal information may be sold on the dark web or used to create fraudulent accounts, apply for loans or credit cards, or engage in other illicit activities, tarnishing victims' reputations and causing long-term damage to their financial stability and creditworthiness.

Beyond the financial ramifications, victims of phishing and scams often experience profound emotional distress. Discovering that they've been deceived and manipulated by malicious actors can lead to feelings of shame, embarrassment, anger, and betrayal. Victims may also experience anxiety and paranoia about the security of their personal information and the potential for further exploitation, impacting their well-being and sense of security in the digital realm.

The aftermath of falling victim to phishing and scams can be time-consuming, stressful, and disruptive. Victims must navigate the complex process of reporting the incident to authorities, notifying financial institutions, and taking steps to mitigate the damage to their finances and personal information. Restoring one's online security and reputation may require considerable effort and resources, including changing passwords, monitoring bank statements, and disputing fraudulent charges, all of which can detract from productivity and peace of mind.

Real-life consequences of phishing and scams extend far beyond financial loss, encompassing emotional distress, compromised personal information, and significant disruptions to victims' lives. It's crucial for individuals to remain vigilant, educate themselves about common phishing tactics, and take proactive measures to protect their sensitive information from falling into the hands of cybercriminals. Additionally, fostering open communication and promoting digital literacy among family members, friends, and colleagues can help prevent future victimization and mitigate the impact of these pervasive online threats.

How to protect your family from Phishing and Scams

Protecting your family from phishing and scams requires a combination of education, awareness, and proactive measures to minimize the risk of falling victim to these online threats. Here are some steps you can take to safeguard your family:

1. **Educate Your Family**: Teach your family members, including children and teens, about the dangers of phishing and scams. Explain common tactics used by cybercriminals, such as deceptive emails, fake websites, and social engineering techniques, and emphasize the importance of skepticism and caution when interacting with unfamiliar messages or requests online.

2. **Promote Digital Literacy**: Foster digital literacy skills among your family members by teaching them how to recognize phishing attempts and scams. Encourage them to verify the authenticity of emails, messages, and websites before clicking on links or providing personal information. Help them understand the importance of keeping their sensitive information secure and practicing good online hygiene.

3. **Use Passkeys and/or Strong Passwords**: Encourage your family to use Passkeys which are meant to be a replacement for Passwords on supported systems. Passkeys are a digital credential that allows users to log in to a website or app without having to enter a username or password. They are a more secure and convenient alternative to passwords. If Passkeys are not supported, use strong, complex, unique passwords for online accounts and avoid sharing them with anyone. Consider using a reputable password manager that also supports passkeys. Use

your password manager to generate and securely store complex passwords for each account, reducing the risk of unauthorized access in the event of a data breach or phishing attack.

4. **Enable Two-Factor Authentication (2FA)**: Enable two-factor authentication (2FA) on your family's online accounts whenever possible. 2FA adds an extra layer of security by requiring users to provide a second form of verification, such as a code sent to their mobile device, in addition to their password, making it more difficult for attackers to gain unauthorized access to accounts. Avoid using SMS or Text based tokens. Instead use an Authenticator app such as Google Authenticator or Microsoft Authenticator.

5. **Install Security Software**: Install reputable antivirus and anti-malware software on your family's devices to help detect and prevent phishing attempts, malware infections, and other online threats. Keep the software up to date to ensure it provides maximum protection against evolving threats.

6. **Update Software Regularly**: Ensure that your family's devices, including computers, smartphones, and tablets, are kept up to date with the latest security patches and software updates. Vulnerabilities in outdated software can be exploited by cybercriminals to launch phishing attacks and infect devices with malware.

7. **Use Secure Connections**: Encourage your family to use secure Wi-Fi networks and encrypted connections, especially when accessing sensitive information or conducting financial transactions online. Avoid using public Wi-Fi networks for sensitive activities, as they may be vulnerable to

interception by attackers.

8. **Stay Informed**: Keep yourself informed about the latest phishing trends and scams by staying up to date on cybersecurity news and advisories. Share relevant information with your family members and discuss any new threats or vulnerabilities that may arise.

9. **Establish Open Communication**: Foster open communication with your family members about their online activities and any concerns they may have about phishing and scams. Encourage them to report suspicious messages or incidents to you or another trusted adult, and provide support and guidance as needed.

By taking proactive steps to educate your family about phishing and scams, promoting good online habits, and implementing security measures to protect their devices and personal information, you can help reduce the risk of falling victim to these pervasive online threats.

CHAPTER 7

Overuse and Addiction

How to Recognize Overuse and Addiction

Recognizing internet overuse and addiction in children can be challenging for parents, but there are several key signs to watch for. Observe changes in behavior and mood. Excessive internet use may lead to irritability, withdrawal from family activities, or a noticeable decline in academic performance. If a child becomes defensive or secretive about their online activities, it could indicate they are hiding the extent of their internet use.

Monitor the amount of time spent online. While it's natural for children to spend time on the internet for schoolwork, socializing, or entertainment, excessive screen time can be a red flag. Keep track of the hours spent online each day and whether it interferes with other aspects of their life, such as sleep, physical activity, or face-to-face social interactions.

Pay attention to physical symptoms that may indicate internet overuse. These can include headaches, eyestrain, and neck or back pain from prolonged periods of sitting and staring at screens. Poor posture and neglect of personal hygiene or nutrition due to excessive internet use are also potential signs.

Finally, observe how your child reacts when internet access is limited. If they become highly agitated, anxious, or even aggressive when asked to take a break from the internet, it may suggest dependence or addiction. Engage in open and non-judgmental conversations with your child about their internet habits and concerns and consider seeking professional help if you suspect they may be struggling with internet addiction.

Real Life Example of Overuse and Addiction

Imagine a family where a once vibrant and outgoing teenager, let's call him Alex, becomes increasingly withdrawn and irritable. His parents notice a significant decline in his grades, and he spends most of his free time locked in his room glued to his computer screen. At first, they chalk it up to typical teenage behavior, but as the situation worsens, they realize it might be something more serious: internet overuse and addiction.

Alex's obsession with online gaming consumes his every waking hour. He stays up late into the night, sacrificing sleep and neglecting other responsibilities. His physical health deteriorates as he rarely leaves his room, leading to weight gain and a decline in personal hygiene. When his parents attempt to limit his internet usage, Alex becomes defensive and lashes out, arguing that he needs to be online to connect with his friends and maintain his virtual identity.

Despite their efforts to intervene, Alex's behavior spirals out of control. He becomes increasingly isolated from real-life social interactions, preferring the anonymity and instant gratification of the online world. His relationships with family and friends suffer, as he prioritizes his virtual life over real-life connections. The once bright future Alex envisioned for himself fades as his academic performance continues to plummet, and his dreams and aspirations take a backseat to his addiction.

Ultimately, Alex's internet overuse and addiction take a toll on his mental and emotional well-being, as well as his quality of life. His parents seek professional help, and through therapy and support groups, Alex begins to understand the root causes of his addiction and learns healthier coping mechanisms. With time and dedication, he gradually breaks free from the grip of his internet addiction and rebuilds his life, reconnecting with his passions, pursuing his academic goals, and rebuilding meaningful relationships with those around him. This real-life example highlights the destructive power of internet overuse and addiction and the importance of early intervention and support in overcoming it.

Consequences of Overuse and Addiction

Internet overuse and addiction can lead to a wide range of consequences, affecting various aspects of an individual's life. There are significant implications for mental health. Excessive internet use can exacerbate feelings of anxiety, depression, and loneliness, particularly if it leads to social isolation and a lack of real-life social interactions. Constant exposure to online content can also contribute to feelings of inadequacy and low self-esteem, especially when comparing oneself to others on social media.

Internet overuse can have detrimental effects on physical health. Prolonged periods of sitting and staring at screens can lead to a sedentary lifestyle, increasing the risk of obesity, cardiovascular problems, and other health issues. Additionally, poor posture and repetitive strain injuries are common among individuals who spend excessive amounts of time on computers, tablets, or smartphones.

There are academic and professional consequences. For students, internet overuse can result in decreased academic performance due to procrastination, distraction, and a lack of focus. It may also impair cognitive abilities such as memory and attention span. In the workplace, excessive internet use can lead to decreased productivity, missed deadlines, and strained relationships with colleagues.

Internet overuse and addiction can have financial implications. Compulsive online shopping, gambling, or gaming can lead to financial problems and debt. Individuals may also neglect their responsibilities, such as paying bills or meeting financial obligations, in favor of spending money on internet-related activities.

There are social consequences to consider. Internet addiction can strain relationships with family and friends, as individuals prioritize online interactions over real-life connections. It may also lead to feelings of alienation and disconnection from the offline world, as individuals become increasingly immersed in virtual environments.

Internet overuse and addiction can have far-reaching consequences, impacting mental, physical, academic, financial, and social well-being. Recognizing the signs of internet addiction and seeking appropriate support and intervention are crucial steps in mitigating these negative effects and promoting healthier internet usage habits.

How to Protect Your Family from Overuse and Addiction

Protecting your family from internet overuse and addiction requires proactive measures and ongoing awareness. Here are some strategies to help safeguard your family's well-being:

1. Establish clear boundaries: Set limits on screen time for each family member, including designated times for device use and breaks. Create a family media plan that outlines rules and expectations regarding internet usage, such as no screens during meals or before bedtime.

2. Lead by example: Be a role model for healthy internet habits by demonstrating moderation and balance in

your own screen time. Engage in offline activities as a family, such as outdoor outings, board games, or creative projects, to show that there are enjoyable alternatives to screen-based entertainment.

3. Foster open communication: Encourage regular conversations about internet use within the family. Create a supportive environment where children feel comfortable discussing their online experiences, concerns, and interests. Be attentive to any signs of distress or addiction and address them promptly and empathetically.

4. Monitor online activities: Keep track of your family's internet usage by utilizing parental control tools and monitoring software. Set up filters and restrictions to block inappropriate content and limit access to certain websites or apps. Regularly review your child's online history and discuss any potential issues or risks that arise.

5. Promote balance and healthy habits: Encourage a balanced lifestyle by emphasizing the importance of physical activity, hobbies, and face-to-face social interactions. Encourage your family to engage in offline activities that promote well-being and personal growth, such as reading, exercising, or pursuing creative interests.

6. Educate about online safety: Teach your family about the potential risks and dangers of the internet, including cyberbullying, online predators, and scams. Emphasize the importance of privacy, security, and responsible digital citizenship. Provide guidance on how to recognize and respond to problematic online behaviors and situations.

7. Seek professional help if needed: If you suspect that

a family member is struggling with internet overuse or addiction, don't hesitate to seek professional assistance. Consult with a mental health professional or addiction specialist who can provide personalized assessment, support, and treatment options tailored to your family's needs.

By implementing these strategies and fostering a healthy relationship with technology, you can help protect your family from internet overuse and addiction while promoting balanced and mindful internet usage habits.

CHAPTER 8

Privacy Concerns

How to Recognize Privacy Concerns

Recognizing privacy concerns online is essential for safeguarding personal information and maintaining digital security. Always be vigilant about the information you share on websites, social media platforms, and other online services. Avoid providing sensitive details such as your full name, address, phone number, or financial information unless absolutely necessary. Be mindful of the privacy settings on social media accounts and adjust them to limit who can see your posts, photos, and personal information.

Pay attention to website privacy policies and terms of service agreements. Many websites collect and track user data for targeted advertising and other purposes. Take the time to read and understand these policies and consider the implications of sharing your data with third-party companies. Look for websites that prioritize transparency and offer clear explanations of how they collect, use, and protect your personal information.

Be cautious when interacting with unknown or unverified sources online. Phishing scams, malware, and identity theft are prevalent threats that can compromise your privacy and security. Avoid clicking on suspicious links or downloading attachments from unfamiliar emails or websites. Use reputable antivirus software and security measures to protect against malware and other online threats.

Regularly review your privacy settings and security measures across all your online accounts and devices. Keep software, operating systems, and security tools up to date to protect against vulnerabilities and exploits. Be proactive in managing your digital footprint by periodically auditing your online presence, removing outdated or unnecessary information, and minimizing the amount of personal data you share online.

By staying informed, cautious, and proactive, you can recognize and address privacy concerns online, helping to protect your personal information and maintain your digital security and privacy.

Real-Life Example of Privacy Violation Online

A real-life example of privacy violation online involves the data breach of Facebook in 2018, where the personal information of millions of users was compromised and exploited without their consent. Cambridge Analytica, a political consulting firm, obtained access to the data of over 87 million Facebook users through an app that collected information from users and their friends. This data was then used for targeted political advertising during the 2016 US presidential election campaign.

The incident highlighted the risks associated with third-party access to personal data on social media platforms and raised concerns about privacy infringement and data misuse. Many Facebook users were unaware that their information was being harvested and used for political purposes, leading to widespread outrage and calls for greater accountability and transparency from tech companies.

The Facebook-Cambridge Analytica scandal underscored the importance of protecting user privacy and prompted increased scrutiny of data practices across the tech industry. It served as a wake-up call for both users and companies to reassess their approach to data privacy and security, and sparked debates about regulations and policies to safeguard personal information online.

This real-life example demonstrates the far-reaching consequences of privacy violations online, affecting individuals' trust in technology platforms and their willingness to share personal information online. It emphasizes the need for stronger privacy protections, greater transparency, and enhanced oversight to prevent similar incidents in the future and ensure that users' privacy rights are respected and upheld in the digital age.

Consequences of Privacy Violations

Privacy violations online can have significant and wide-ranging consequences for individuals, organizations, and society as a whole. There are personal ramifications. When personal information is exposed without consent, individuals may experience feelings of violation, vulnerability, and loss of control over their own data. This breach of privacy can lead to emotional distress, anxiety, and distrust of online platforms and services.

Sensitive information such as financial data or medical records being compromised can result in identity theft, financial fraud, or even blackmail, causing serious harm to individuals' financial well-being and reputation.

Privacy violations can have social repercussions. When personal data is misused or exploited, it can damage relationships and erode trust between individuals, businesses, and institutions. Online harassment, stalking, or doxxing – the malicious release of personal information – can lead to real-world safety concerns and harm individuals' sense of security and privacy.

When data breaches occur within organizations or government agencies, it can undermine public confidence in institutions and their ability to safeguard sensitive information, leading to erosion of trust and accountability.

There are legal and regulatory implications. Organizations that fail to adequately protect user data may face legal consequences, including fines, lawsuits, and reputational damage. Regulatory bodies such as the European Union's General Data Protection Regulation (GDPR) and the California Consumer Privacy Act (CCPA) impose strict requirements on how companies collect, process, and store personal data, and violations can result in severe penalties. Compliance with these regulations is not only essential for avoiding legal repercussions but also for maintaining trust and credibility with customers and stakeholders.

Finally, there are economic impacts. Data breaches and privacy violations can incur significant financial costs for affected individuals and organizations. Companies may suffer financial losses due to fines, legal fees, and remediation efforts, as well as damage to their brand reputation and customer loyalty. Additionally, the broader economy may be affected by decreased consumer confidence in online services and e-commerce platforms, leading to reduced online activity and spending.

The consequences of privacy violations online are far-reaching and multifaceted, affecting individuals' well-being, social trust, legal compliance, and economic prosperity. Protecting privacy rights and implementing robust security measures are essential for mitigating these risks and fostering a safe and trustworthy digital environment.

How to protect your family from privacy violations

Protecting your family from privacy violations online requires a combination of awareness, proactive measures, and ongoing vigilance. Here are some strategies to help safeguard your family's privacy in the digital world:

1. Educate your family about online privacy: Start

by discussing the importance of privacy and the potential risks of sharing personal information online. Teach your family members about common privacy threats, such as phishing scams, identity theft, and data breaches. Encourage them to be cautious about the information they share online and to think twice before disclosing sensitive details.

2. Use privacy settings and security features: Take advantage of privacy settings and security features offered by online platforms, social media sites, and devices. Configure privacy settings to limit the visibility of personal information and control who can access your family's content and data. Enable two-factor authentication and use strong, unique passwords to protect accounts from unauthorized access.

3. Practice safe browsing habits: Teach your family members to practice safe browsing habits when navigating the internet. Encourage them to verify the legitimacy of websites before sharing any personal information or making online purchases. Install ad blockers and browser extensions that can help prevent tracking and minimize exposure to malicious content.

4. Limit exposure of personal information: Minimize the amount of personal information you and your family members share online. Avoid oversharing on social media and be cautious when posting photos, location data, or other identifying details. Consider using pseudonyms or aliases instead of real names, especially for accounts or forums frequented by children and teenagers.

5. Regularly review privacy settings and permissions: Periodically review the privacy settings and

permissions of apps, websites, and online services used by your family. Remove any unnecessary permissions or access rights that may compromise privacy or security. Stay informed about updates and changes to privacy policies and terms of service and adjust settings accordingly.

6. Use encryption and secure communication tools: Utilize encryption and secure communication tools to protect sensitive information and messages exchanged online. Encourage your family to use encrypted messaging apps, virtual private networks (VPNs), and secure email services to safeguard their privacy and confidentiality.

7. Keep software and devices up to date: Ensure that all devices and software applications used by your family members are kept up to date with the latest security patches and updates. Regularly check for software updates and install them promptly to address any security vulnerabilities and protect against known threats.

By implementing these strategies and fostering a culture of privacy awareness within your family, you can help protect your loved ones from privacy violations online and empower them to navigate the digital world safely and responsibly.

CHAPTER 9

CyberSecurity Threats

Recognizing cybersecurity threats is essential in today's digital age to protect yourself and your family from online dangers. One of the key indicators of a cybersecurity threat is receiving unsolicited emails or messages that appear suspicious. These messages often contain spelling or grammatical errors, ask for sensitive information like passwords or financial details, or pressure you to click on links or download attachments. Such attempts are often phishing attacks designed to trick you into revealing personal information or installing malware on your device.

Another way to recognize cybersecurity threats is by monitoring your online accounts for unusual activity. Keep an eye out for unfamiliar logins, changes to account settings, or unrecognized transactions. Enable notifications for login attempts or account changes to quickly detect and respond to potential security breaches. Additionally, be cautious of unexpected pop-up windows, notifications, or alerts while browsing the internet or using apps. These could be signs of malware infection, phishing scams, or fraudulent advertisements attempting to compromise your device or steal your data.

Pay attention to the behavior of websites you visit as well.

Be cautious of sites that display unusual behavior, such as frequent redirects, unexpected downloads, or warnings about security risks. Look for signs of a secure connection, such as HTTPS encryption and a padlock icon in the browser's address bar, before entering any sensitive information. Additionally, be wary of unexplained performance issues on your devices, such as slowdowns, crashes, or unexpected changes in settings. These could be indicators of malware infection or other security threats compromising the performance and stability of your system.

Stay alert to social engineering tactics used by cybercriminals to manipulate or deceive individuals into revealing sensitive information or performing risky actions. This could include impersonating trusted entities, such as tech support representatives or government agencies, to trick you into providing passwords, financial details, or access to your devices. Additionally, stay informed about data breaches and security incidents affecting organizations or online services you use. Monitor news reports, security advisories, and breach notification emails to stay updated on potential risks and take appropriate action, such as changing passwords or enabling additional security measures.

By remaining vigilant and recognizing these common cybersecurity threats, you can take proactive steps to protect yourself and your family from online security risks. Implementing strong security practices, staying informed about potential threats, and maintaining a cautious approach to online interactions are essential for safeguarding your digital safety and privacy in today's interconnected world.

Real Life Example of Cyber Security Breach

One of the most notable real-life examples of a cybersecurity breach occurred in 2017 with the Equifax data breach. Equifax, one of the largest consumer credit reporting agencies in the United States, experienced a massive breach that compromised the personal information of approximately 147 million individuals.

The breach exposed sensitive personal data, including names, Social Security numbers, birth dates, addresses, and in some cases, driver's license numbers. This extensive breach affected a significant portion of the American population and raised serious concerns about the security of personal information held by major corporations.

The Equifax breach was particularly concerning due to the nature of the data compromised. Social Security numbers are key pieces of information used for identity verification, and their exposure in this breach put millions of individuals at risk of identity theft, financial fraud, and other forms of cybercrime.

The fallout from the Equifax breach was far-reaching and resulted in widespread public outrage, congressional hearings, and regulatory scrutiny. Equifax faced numerous lawsuits, investigations by government agencies, and significant financial penalties. The breach also prompted calls for stronger cybersecurity regulations and greater accountability for companies responsible for safeguarding sensitive consumer data.

The Equifax data breach serves as a stark reminder of the serious consequences of cybersecurity failures and the importance of implementing robust security measures to protect personal information. It underscores the need for organizations to prioritize cybersecurity best practices, invest in advanced threat detection and prevention technologies, and maintain transparency and accountability in handling sensitive data. Additionally, it highlights the critical role of individuals in safeguarding their own personal information by remaining vigilant against potential threats and taking proactive steps to protect their digital identities.

Consequences of Cybersecurity Threats

Cybersecurity threats can have significant and far-reaching

consequences, impacting individuals, organizations, and society as a whole. Here are several key consequences:

1. Financial losses: Cybersecurity breaches can result in substantial financial losses for individuals and businesses. Cybercriminals may steal sensitive financial information, such as credit card numbers or bank account details, leading to unauthorized transactions, identity theft, and fraud. Additionally, organizations may incur costs related to incident response, remediation, and legal fees, as well as potential fines and penalties for non-compliance with data protection regulations.

2. Damage to reputation and trust: A cybersecurity breach can severely damage an organization's reputation and erode customer trust. News of a data breach can undermine confidence in the affected company's ability to protect sensitive information, leading to the loss of customers, partners, and investors. Reputational damage may have long-term consequences for the organization's brand image and competitiveness in the marketplace.

3. Disruption of operations: Cybersecurity threats, such as malware infections or distributed denial-of-service (DDoS) attacks, can disrupt normal business operations and cause downtime. This can result in lost productivity, missed deadlines, and delays in delivering products or services to customers. In some cases, organizations may be forced to temporarily shut down systems or networks to contain the threat and prevent further damage, leading to financial losses and reputational harm.

4. Legal and regulatory consequences: Organizations that experience cybersecurity breaches may face legal and regulatory consequences, especially if they fail to

protect sensitive data or comply with data protection laws. Depending on the jurisdiction and the nature of the breach, companies may be subject to fines, lawsuits, and regulatory sanctions. Compliance with data breach notification requirements and other legal obligations can also impose additional costs and administrative burdens on affected organizations.

5. Intellectual property theft: Cybersecurity threats pose a risk to intellectual property (IP) assets, such as trade secrets, patents, and proprietary technology. Cybercriminals may target organizations to steal valuable IP for economic gain or competitive advantage. The theft of sensitive research, product designs, or other proprietary information can have serious implications for innovation, market competitiveness, and business success.

6. Impact on critical infrastructure: Cybersecurity threats targeting critical infrastructure, such as power grids, transportation systems, and healthcare facilities, can have devastating consequences for public safety and national security. Cyberattacks on critical infrastructure can disrupt essential services, cause widespread chaos and confusion, and pose significant risks to human life and well-being. Protecting critical infrastructure from cyber threats is paramount to ensuring the resilience and security of society as a whole.

7. Psychological and emotional impact: Individuals who fall victim to cybercrime may experience psychological and emotional distress, including feelings of violation, anxiety, and helplessness. Identity theft, online harassment, or cyberstalking can have profound effects on victims' mental health and well-being, leading to stress, depression,

and social isolation. The psychological impact of cyberattacks extends beyond the immediate financial and operational consequences and underscores the need for comprehensive support and resources for affected individuals.

Cybersecurity threats pose serious risks to individuals, organizations, and society, emphasizing the importance of proactive cybersecurity measures, robust risk management practices, and collaborative efforts to address evolving cyber threats effectively.

How to Protect Your Family from Cybersecurity Threats

Protecting your family from cybersecurity threats is crucial in today's digital world. Here are several steps you can take to enhance your family's online security:

1. Educate your family about cybersecurity: Start by discussing the importance of cybersecurity and the potential risks of online threats, such as phishing scams, malware infections, and identity theft. Teach your family members how to recognize suspicious emails, links, and websites, and emphasize the importance of safe online behavior, such as using strong, unique passwords and avoiding sharing personal information with strangers.

2. Use strong passwords and enable multi-factor authentication (MFA): Encourage your family members to use strong, unique passwords for their online accounts and enable MFA whenever possible. Consider using a password manager to securely store and manage passwords for multiple accounts, reducing the risk of password-related breaches.

3. Keep software and devices up to date: Regularly update all devices and software applications used by your family, including computers, smartphones,

tablets, and internet-connected devices (IoT). Software updates often include security patches and bug fixes that address known vulnerabilities and help protect against cyber threats.

4. Install antivirus and security software: Install reputable antivirus and security software on all devices to help detect and prevent malware infections, phishing attempts, and other online threats. Keep the software up to date and configure regular scans to ensure ongoing protection against emerging threats.

5. Secure your home network: Secure your home Wi-Fi network by using strong, unique passwords for your router and enabling encryption (such as WPA2 or WPA3). Consider setting up a guest network for visitors and IoT devices to isolate them from your main network and reduce the risk of unauthorized access.

6. Practice safe browsing habits: Teach your family members to practice safe browsing habits when using the internet. Encourage them to verify the legitimacy of websites before entering sensitive information, avoid clicking on suspicious links or ads, and use browser extensions or plugins that block malicious content and protect against tracking.

7. Monitor online activity: Regularly monitor your family's online activity and review privacy settings on social media accounts, apps, and online services. Keep an eye out for any signs of unusual or suspicious behavior, such as unauthorized access to accounts or unfamiliar devices connected to your network.

8. Communicate openly about cybersecurity: Foster an open dialogue about cybersecurity within

your family, encouraging communication and collaboration to address potential threats and concerns. Encourage your family members to report any suspicious activity or security incidents promptly and provide guidance and support in responding to cyber threats effectively.

By implementing these proactive measures and fostering a culture of cybersecurity awareness within your family, you can help protect your loved ones from online threats and empower them to navigate the digital world safely and securely.

CHAPTER 10

Social Media

Importance and Potential Risks of Social Media

Social media holds immense importance in the lives of today's youth due to its ability to foster communication, connection, and community. Through platforms like Instagram, Snapchat, and TikTok, young people can effortlessly stay in touch with friends, family, and peers, transcending geographical barriers. This constant connectivity helps alleviate feelings of isolation and loneliness, especially in an increasingly digital world where face-to-face interactions may be limited. Social media offers a virtual space where youth can share their experiences, thoughts, and emotions, creating a sense of belonging and support.

Social media serves as a platform for self-expression and creativity, allowing youth to showcase their talents, interests, and unique identities to a global audience. From crafting visually stunning Instagram posts to sharing original music on SoundCloud, young people use social media as a digital canvas to express themselves authentically and find validation and recognition from their peers. This freedom of expression fosters creativity, confidence, and self-discovery among youth as they navigate the complexities of adolescence.

Social media plays a pivotal role in shaping youth culture and facilitating social change. Platforms like Twitter and Facebook have become powerful tools for activism, enabling young people to mobilize around important social issues, raise awareness, and drive meaningful change. From organizing protests against racial injustice to advocating for climate action, youth-led movements leverage social media to amplify their voices, connect with like-minded individuals, and hold institutions accountable. Social media empowers young people to become agents of change and contribute to building a more just and equitable society.

Additionally, social media serves as a gateway to information and learning, providing youth with access to a wealth of educational resources, news articles, and online communities. From following educational influencers on YouTube to participating in discussion forums on Reddit, young people use social media to expand their knowledge, explore new ideas, and engage in intellectual discourse. This informal learning environment encourages curiosity, critical thinking, and lifelong learning, complementing traditional educational experiences and empowering youth to pursue their passions and interests.

In conclusion, social media is of paramount importance to today's youth as it facilitates communication, fosters self-expression and creativity, drives social change, and provides access to information and learning opportunities. While social media offers numerous benefits and opportunities for youth, it is essential for them to navigate these platforms mindfully, mindful of the potential risks and challenges associated with online interactions. With responsible use and digital literacy skills, young people can harness the power of social media to enrich their lives and make a positive impact on the world around them.

The pervasive presence of social media in the lives of today's youth brings with it a host of potential risks and challenges that must be navigated with caution. One significant risk is the impact on mental health and well-being. Constant exposure to carefully curated and often unrealistic portrayals of life on social media can lead to feelings of inadequacy, low self-esteem, and body image issues among young people. The pressure to conform to unrealistic beauty standards or portray a perfect image online can contribute to anxiety, depression, and other mental health problems, especially when coupled with cyberbullying and online harassment.

Social media can exacerbate social isolation and loneliness despite its promise of connectivity. The superficial nature of online interactions may lead to a lack of meaningful connections and a sense of disconnection from real-life relationships. Excessive use of social media can also interfere with offline socializing and interpersonal communication skills, leading to feelings of loneliness and social anxiety among young people who rely heavily on digital interactions for social validation and approval.

Another significant risk associated with social media for today's youth is the potential for privacy breaches and online safety concerns. Young people may inadvertently share sensitive personal information or engage in risky online behaviors, such as meeting strangers or sharing intimate photos, which can leave them vulnerable to exploitation, cyberbullying, and online predators.

The data collected by social media platforms for targeted advertising and personalization purposes raises concerns about privacy violations and unauthorized access to personal information, posing risks to young people's digital identities and security.

Social media can contribute to addictive behaviors and poor digital habits among young people, leading to issues with impulse control, attention span, and productivity. The dopamine-driven feedback loop of likes, comments, and shares on social media platforms can create a compulsive need for validation and constant engagement, resulting in excessive screen time, sleep disturbances, and neglect of real-life responsibilities. The addictive nature of social media can also exacerbate feelings of FOMO (fear of missing out) and contribute to a constant state of distraction and dissatisfaction among youth.

While social media offers numerous benefits and opportunities for today's youth, it also presents significant risks to their mental health, privacy, online safety, and well-being. It is essential for parents, caregivers, educators, and policymakers to address these risks proactively by promoting digital literacy, fostering healthy online habits, and providing support and resources to help young people navigate the complexities of the digital world responsibly. With awareness, education, and support, young people can harness the positive aspects of social media while mitigating its potential harms.

Staying Vigilant

Staying vigilant of family social media usage is essential for parents in today's digital age. One crucial step is to establish open communication and trust with children regarding their online activities. Parents should maintain regular conversations with their children about their social media use, including the platforms they frequent, the content they consume, and the interactions they have online. By fostering a supportive and non-judgmental environment, parents can encourage children to share any concerns or issues they encounter on social media, enabling them to address potential risks and challenges together.

Additionally, parents should actively monitor their children's social media accounts and online interactions while respecting their privacy and autonomy. This includes regularly reviewing privacy settings and security measures on social media platforms, monitoring children's friend lists and followers, and checking their online activity and posts for any signs of inappropriate content or behavior. Parents can also use parental control tools and monitoring software to track their children's online activities and set limits on screen time, ensuring a healthy balance between online and offline activities.

Parents should educate themselves about the various risks and dangers associated with social media, including cyberbullying, online predators, privacy violations, and addictive behaviors. By staying informed about emerging trends and threats in the digital landscape, parents can better support their children in navigating social media responsibly and safely. They can also provide guidance on how to recognize and respond to problematic situations online, such as cyberbullying or inappropriate requests from strangers.

Parents should lead by example and model positive digital behaviors for their children. By demonstrating responsible social media use, setting boundaries around screen time, and prioritizing face-to-face interactions and offline activities as a family, parents can instill healthy habits and values in their children. Creating a technology-free zone during mealtimes or before bedtime can help foster meaningful connections and promote a balanced lifestyle.

In conclusion, staying vigilant of family social media usage requires proactive involvement, open communication, and ongoing education. By establishing trust, monitoring online activities, educating themselves and their children about potential risks, and modeling positive digital behaviors, parents can help ensure that their family navigates social media safely and responsibly. With parental guidance and support, children can develop the skills and resilience needed to thrive in the digital world while minimizing the potential harms associated with social media.

CHAPTER 11

Nightmare IRL: Discord and Telegram

Discord is a popular messaging and voice chat platform designed primarily for gamers, although it has expanded to cater to various communities and interests beyond gaming. Users can create servers, which are essentially chat rooms, where they can communicate via text, voice, and video. Discord offers features such as direct messaging, voice channels, file sharing, and integration with other platforms like Twitch and YouTube.

While Discord itself isn't inherently dangerous, there are potential risks associated with its use, as with any online platform:

1.**Privacy concerns**: Users should be cautious about sharing personal information on Discord, as with any online platform. There have been instances of privacy breaches, hacking, and doxxing (revealing personal information about individuals) on Discord.

2.**Inappropriate content**: Discord servers can be created and moderated by anyone, so there's a risk of encountering inappropriate or offensive content, including hate speech, explicit material, or discussions promoting harmful behaviors.

3. **Cyberbullying and harassment**: Like any online community, Discord can be susceptible to cyberbullying and harassment. Users may encounter abusive behavior, trolling, or targeted harassment in servers or direct messages.

4. **Malware and phishing**: As with any online platform, users should be wary of links or files shared on Discord, as they could potentially contain malware or lead to phishing attempts aimed at stealing personal information or login credentials.

5. **Predatory behavior**: Discord, like other social platforms, can be used by individuals with malicious intent to prey on vulnerable users, particularly minors. Parents and guardians should be aware of who their children are communicating with on Discord and take appropriate precautions.

Discord and Telegram are popular messaging apps that facilitate communication among users through text, voice, and video. While both platforms offer unique features that promote community engagement and instant messaging, they also come with inherent risks that users should be aware of. The dangers associated with these apps can range from privacy concerns to potential exposure to harmful content, which can have real-life implications, particularly for younger users.

Privacy and Data Security Risks

One of the primary dangers of using Discord and Telegram is related to privacy and data security. Discord has faced scrutiny over its data collection practices, where user data can potentially be accessed by third parties. Telegram, while known for its strong encryption features, has also had vulnerabilities that could expose users to data breaches. In both cases, users often share personal information without fully understanding how it might be used or misused, leading to risks of identity theft or harassment.

Exposure to Inappropriate Content

Both platforms can be gateways to inappropriate or harmful content, especially for younger users. Discord's server-based model allows for the creation of communities that may not be adequately moderated. As a result, users might encounter hate speech, graphic content, or even predatory behavior. Similarly, Telegram's channels can host explicit material, promoting illegal activities such as drug sales or extremist ideologies. The lack of strict content moderation can lead to significant psychological impacts on vulnerable users.

Cyberbullying and Harassment

Cyberbullying is another serious issue on both Discord and Telegram. The anonymity provided by these platforms can embolden individuals to engage in harassment or bullying behaviors without fear of repercussion. Victims may experience emotional distress, leading to real-life implications such as anxiety, depression, and even suicidal thoughts. The communal nature of these apps can amplify the impact, as harassment can occur in public channels where many others can witness or participate in the behavior.

Misinformation and Radicalization

Both Discord and Telegram have been used as tools for spreading misinformation and fostering radicalization. Discord's various communities can be exploited to propagate false information or conspiracy theories, impacting users' perceptions of reality. On Telegram, extremist groups often utilize the platform to recruit members, share propaganda, and coordinate activities. This environment can contribute to societal polarization and increase the risk of individuals engaging in dangerous behaviors influenced by extremist ideologies.

Lack of Regulation and Accountability

The relative lack of regulation governing Discord and Telegram poses significant risks. Unlike more traditional social media platforms, these apps often operate with minimal oversight, making it challenging to enforce community guidelines or protect users effectively. This lack of accountability can lead to a culture where harmful behaviors are normalized, leaving users feeling vulnerable and unsupported. As a result, individuals may struggle to seek help when facing issues such as harassment or exposure to harmful content.

While Discord and Telegram offer valuable communication tools, the dangers associated with their use cannot be overlooked. From privacy risks and exposure to inappropriate content to cyberbullying and misinformation, the real-life implications for users can be profound. As these platforms continue to evolve, it is crucial for users—especially younger ones—to be aware of these dangers and take proactive steps to protect themselves. Awareness, education, and advocacy for better moderation practices can help mitigate some of these risks and foster a safer online environment.

CHAPTER 12

Keeping Your Family Safe

Practical Questions and Answers

How can parents ensure that the devices their children use are secure, and what steps can they take to prevent unauthorized access or cyberattacks?

Parents can take several steps to ensure that the devices their children use are secure and to prevent unauthorized access or cyberattacks:

1. **Use Strong Passwords**: Encourage your children to use strong, unique passwords for their devices and online accounts. Use a password manager to securely store and manage passwords. Ideally a hardware device such as a Yubike or proximity token device along with a password manager for added security.

2. **Enable Device Locks**: Set up PINs, passwords, or biometric authentication (such as fingerprint or facial recognition) to lock devices when they're not in use. This helps prevent unauthorized access in case the device is lost or stolen.

3. **Update Software Regularly**: Ensure that the operating systems, apps, and security software on your children's devices are up to date. Updates often include patches for security vulnerabilities, so keeping devices updated is crucial for maintaining security. Don't rely on automated updates. I've found many times where people set up their systems for automated patching and they are still out of date. Always manually check for patches, reboot and keep checking until no more updates are found with the OS AND applications. Consider using a separate more secure device with limited apps and functionality for online banking or other sensitive tasks. At the start of your day, before browsing the Internet, click on help, about and update to ensure the browser is patched with the latest security updates and restart the browser when done to apply the latest patches. Many new threats are targeting security flaws in popular web browsers such as Chrome and Firefox. Follow this process for any apps or software you use for business, meetings with Zoom or other sensitive tasks.

4. **Install Security Software**: Consider installing reputable antivirus and anti-malware software on your children's devices to detect and remove malicious software. Many security software options also offer features such as web filtering and parental controls. Consider installing a modern firewall with advanced filtering and blocking called intrusion detection system capabilities (IDS) and intrusion prevention system (IPS). Block communications with countries outside of the United States (US).

5. **Use Parental Control Software**: Utilize parental control software to monitor and manage your children's online activities. These tools allow you to set limits on screen time, block inappropriate

content, and track your children's online behavior.

6. **Educate Your Children**: Teach your children about the importance of cybersecurity and safe online practices. Remind them not to answer unknown calls, click on suspicious links in email, text or download files from unknown sources, and encourage them to report any suspicious activity or messages to you.

7. **Secure Internet Connections**: Ensure that your home Wi-Fi network is secured with a strong, unique password and encryption. Setup separate guest, work and home networks for your children's devices to minimize the risk of unauthorized access to your main network.

8. **Enable Two-Factor Authentication**: Enable two-factor authentication (2FA) using a software authenticator app such as Google Authenticator or Microsoft Authenticator. Do NOT use SMS text for MFA whenever possible. This adds an extra layer of security by requiring a second form of verification, such as a code, in addition to their password.

9. **Regularly Back Up Data**: Encourage your children to regularly back up their important files and data to a secure location, such as cloud storage and/or an external hard drive. At least two different backups are recommended. This helps protect against data loss in the event of a cyberattack or device failure. Test and verify your backups at least monthly.

ADDITIONAL CYBER TIPS TO KEEP YOU AND YOUR FAMILY SAFE

1. Use a Password manager and use passkeys in favor of passwords wherever possible.
2. Setup an account with Experian, Equifax, and Transunion - Freeze your credit AND place a 1-year fraud alert.
3. Setup credit monitoring with more than one company such as ID Shield and CreditSecure with Amex
4. Most credit monitoring services include a scan of the dark web and ability to remove your personal information from background check agencies. Use this feature asap to reduce your risk footprint.
5. Scan the dark web with https://haveibeenpwned.com/
6. Setup a Login.gov account with Google / Microsoft Authenticator
7. Setup a mySSN account with ssa.gov with Google / Microsoft Authenticator
8. Setup MFA wherever possible with Google / Microsoft Authenticator - Avoid using SMS text when possible.

9. Place a PIN on your account with you cell phone provider
10. Put any property deeds into a Trust instead of your personal name(s)
11. Constantly monitor your credit and checking accounts for suspicious transactions
12. Setup a separate card and/or account with a small balance to use online
13. Use keystroke encryption on your devices
14. Use PTG Managed Security Services such as XDR and MNDR to detect and block anything suspicious
15. Use PTG encrypted email and data systems
16. Signup for a USPS account to manage your street address
17. Submit a Google Maps Updated Listing that blurs your street address.

By implementing these security measures and promoting good cybersecurity habits, parents can help protect their children's devices and personal information from unauthorized access and cyberattacks.

How can parents stay informed about the latest cybersecurity threats targeting children and teens, and what proactive measures can they take to stay ahead of potential risks?

To stay informed about the latest cybersecurity threats targeting children and teens, parents can take several proactive measures:

1. **Subscribe to Reliable Sources**: Sign up for newsletters, blogs, podcasts and alerts from reputable organizations, such as CISA and websites that specialize in child and teen online safety. These sources often provide updates on emerging threats, tips for staying safe online, and resources for parents.

2. **Follow social media and Online Forums**: Join online communities or follow social media accounts dedicated to cybersecurity and parenting. These platforms can be valuable sources of information and discussion about current trends and challenges in online safety.

3. **Attend Workshops and Webinars**: Look for workshops, webinars, or seminars in your community or online that focus on cybersecurity for families. These events often provide practical advice, expert insights, and opportunities to ask questions about specific concerns.

4. **Stay Connected with Schools and Educators**: Stay in touch with your child's school or educators to learn about any cybersecurity initiatives or educational programs they offer. Schools may provide resources or workshops for parents on topics like online safety, cyberbullying, and digital citizenship.

5. **Utilize Parental Control Software**: Invest in parental control software that offers features such as content filtering, activity monitoring, and app management. Many of these tools also provide alerts or reports on your child's online activities, helping you stay informed about their digital behavior.

6. **Regularly Discuss Online Safety**: Have regular conversations with your children about online safety and cybersecurity. Encourage open communication and create a safe space for them to share any concerns or questions they may have about their online experiences.

7. **Review Privacy Settings**: Regularly review and update privacy settings on your child's devices, apps, and social media accounts. Ensure that privacy settings are configured to limit the amount of

personal information shared online and to restrict access to strangers.

8. **Teach Critical Thinking Skills**: Teach your children critical thinking skills to help them identify and respond to potential online threats independently. Encourage them to question the legitimacy of messages, links, or requests they receive online and to seek help if they're unsure.

9. **Stay Engaged and Involved**: Stay actively involved in your child's online activities by participating in their digital experiences, playing online games together, or exploring websites and apps together. This allows you to stay informed about their online habits and interests while also building trust and rapport.

10. **Lead by Example**: Model safe and responsible online behavior yourself. Show your children how to navigate the internet safely, respect others' privacy, and protect their personal information online.

By staying informed, engaging with your children about online safety, and taking proactive measures to mitigate risks, parents can help protect their children from cybersecurity threats and empower them to navigate the digital world safely and responsibly.

What role do social media platforms play in the online safety of children and teens, and how can parents navigate and mitigate the associated risks?

Social media platforms play a significant role in the online safety of children and teens, as they provide avenues for communication, connection, and self-expression. However, they also present various risks that parents need to navigate and mitigate effectively. Here's how social media platforms impact online safety and what parents can do to address associated risks:

Potential Risks:

- **Cyberbullying**: Social media platforms can be breeding grounds for cyberbullying, where children and teens may face harassment, intimidation, or exclusion from peers.
- **Inappropriate Content**: Children and teens may encounter inappropriate content such as explicit images, violence, or hate speech on social media platforms.
- **Privacy Concerns**: Social media platforms often require users to share personal information, raising concerns about privacy and data security.
- **Predators and Grooming**: Predators may use social media to groom and exploit children and teens, posing as peers or befriending them to gain their trust.

Parental Involvement:

- **Open Communication**: Encourage open communication with your children about their social media use. Discuss potential risks, set guidelines for responsible use, and establish trust so that your children feel comfortable coming to you with any concerns.
- **Set Boundaries**: Establish clear rules and boundaries for social media use, including guidelines on privacy settings, who they can connect with, and what type of content is appropriate to share.
- **Monitor Activity**: Monitor your children's social media activity, either by following them on social media or using parental control software that offers monitoring features. Regularly review their

posts, messages, and interactions for any signs of cyberbullying or inappropriate behavior.

- **Teach Digital Literacy**: Educate your children about the importance of digital literacy and critical thinking skills. Teach them how to evaluate the credibility of information online, spot potential scams or predators, and protect their personal information.

- **Model Positive Behavior**: Set a positive example by demonstrating responsible social media use yourself. Show your children how to engage respectfully with others, protect their privacy, and use social media as a tool for positive communication and connection.

Privacy and Security Measures:

- **Privacy Settings**: Help your children set up and configure privacy settings on their social media accounts to control who can see their posts, messages, and personal information.

- **Two-Factor Authentication**: Encourage your children to enable two-factor authentication on their social media accounts for an added layer of security.

- **Report and Block**: Teach your children how to report and block users who engage in cyberbullying, harassment, or inappropriate behavior on social media platforms.

Educate about Online Safety:

- **Online Safety Education**: Provide your children with age-appropriate education about online safety, including discussions about privacy, security, cyberbullying, and responsible social media use.

- **Stay Informed**: Stay informed about the latest trends and challenges in social media and online safety to better support and guide your children in navigating the digital world.

By actively engaging with your children about social media use, setting clear boundaries, monitoring their activity, and providing guidance on privacy and security measures, parents can help mitigate the risks associated with social media and promote a safer and more positive online experience for their children and teens.

What measures should be taken to secure personal information, such as addresses and school details, on devices and online platforms used by children?

Securing personal information, such as addresses and school details, on devices and online platforms used by children is crucial for protecting their privacy and safety. Here are some measures parents can take to ensure that personal information remains secure:

1. **Educate Your Children**: Teach your children about the importance of safeguarding their personal information, including their full name, address, phone number, school name, and other sensitive details. Explain why it's essential to keep this information private and not share it with strangers online.

2. **Use Privacy Settings**: Ensure that privacy settings are enabled and configured correctly on your children's devices, apps, and online platforms. This includes setting strict privacy controls on social media accounts, restricting access to personal information, and limiting who can view or contact your child online. If you use Apple devices, please visit https://support.apple.com/en-us/105121 for a guide on how to enable privacy and parental controls. Google has a feature called Family Link https://

families.google/familylink/

3. **Review App Permissions**: Regularly review and manage app permissions on your children's devices. Disable unnecessary permissions that could potentially access or share personal information without their consent.

4. **Choose Secure Passkeys/Passwords**: Encourage your children to use Passkeys which are meant to be a replacement for Passwords on supported systems. Passkeys are a digital credential that allows users to log in to a website or app without having to enter a username or password. They are a more secure and convenient alternative to passwords. If Passkeys are not supported, use strong, complex, unique passwords for online accounts and avoid sharing them with anyone. Consider using a reputable password manager that also supports passkeys. Use your password manager to generate and securely store complex passwords for each account, reducing the risk of unauthorized access in the event of a data breach or phishing attack.

5. **Enable Two-Factor Authentication**: Enable two-factor authentication (2FA) on your children's accounts whenever possible. This adds an extra layer of security by requiring a second form of verification, such as a code sent to their phone, in addition to their password.

6. **Avoid Public Wi-Fi Networks**: Advise your children to avoid connecting to public Wi-Fi networks, as these networks may not be secure and could potentially expose their personal information to hackers or cybercriminals.

7. **Public Charging Stations and Cables:** Never use

public charging stations or usb cables to charge your devices. USB Cables like this have been found to be able to inject spyware into mobile devices and tablets.

8. **Regularly Update Software**: Ensure that the operating systems, apps, and security software on your children's devices are kept up to date with the latest security patches and updates. This helps protect against vulnerabilities that could be exploited to access personal information.

9. **Teach Safe Browsing Habits**: Teach your children safe browsing habits, such as avoiding clicking on suspicious links or downloading files from unknown sources. Encourage them to stick to reputable websites and to be cautious when sharing personal information online.

10. **Monitor Online Activity**: Monitor your children's online activity and interactions, both on their devices and on social media platforms. Stay vigilant for any signs of potential privacy breaches or unauthorized sharing of personal information.

11. **Create a Family Privacy Policy**: Establish clear rules and guidelines within your family about how personal information should be handled and shared online. Encourage open communication and create a safe environment where your children feel comfortable coming to you with any privacy concerns.

By implementing these measures and fostering a culture of privacy and security within your family, you can help protect your children's personal information and minimize the risk of privacy breaches or identity theft.

How can parents strike a balance between allowing their

children to explore and learn in the digital world while ensuring their safety and privacy are prioritized?

Striking a balance between allowing children to explore and learn in the digital world while prioritizing their safety and privacy requires a thoughtful and proactive approach. Here are some strategies parents can use to achieve this balance:

1. **Set Clear Boundaries and Guidelines**: Establish clear rules and guidelines for your children's online activities, including limits on screen time, appropriate content, and safe behavior. Clearly communicate your expectations and the reasons behind them to help your children understand the importance of safety and privacy.

2. **Encourage Open Communication**: Foster open communication with your children about their online experiences. Create a supportive environment where they feel comfortable discussing their interests, concerns, and any challenges they encounter online. Encourage them to come to you with questions or if they encounter anything that makes them feel uncomfortable or unsafe.

3. **Educate About Online Safety**: Provide your children with age-appropriate education about online safety and privacy. Teach them about the risks and challenges of the digital world, including cyberbullying, online predators, phishing scams, and the importance of protecting their personal information. Empower them with the knowledge and skills they need to navigate the internet safely and responsibly.

4. **Model Responsible Behavior**: Lead by example by demonstrating responsible digital habits yourself. Show your children how to use technology mindfully,

respect others' privacy, and prioritize safety and security online. Be mindful of your own screen time and digital use, as children often emulate the behavior of their parents.

5. **Use Parental Controls and Monitoring Tools**: Utilize parental control software and monitoring tools to help manage your children's online activities and ensure their safety. These tools can help you set limits on screen time, block inappropriate content, monitor their online interactions, and track their digital behavior. However, remember to balance monitoring with trust and respect for your children's privacy.

6. **Teach Critical Thinking Skills**: Teach your children critical thinking skills to help them evaluate the credibility and reliability of information they encounter online. Encourage them to question what they see and read, think critically about online content, and consider the potential consequences of their actions online.

7. **Encourage Offline Activities**: Encourage your children to engage in a variety of offline activities, hobbies, and interests that promote creativity, social interaction, and physical activity. Help them find a balance between online and offline pursuits to support their well-being and development.

8. **Stay Informed and Involved**: Stay informed about the latest trends, apps, and challenges in the digital world. Stay involved in your children's online activities by regularly checking in with them, reviewing their online behavior, and staying up to date with the platforms and apps they use. Be proactive in addressing any safety or privacy concerns that arise.

By implementing these strategies and maintaining an ongoing dialogue with your children about online safety and privacy, you can help them explore and learn in the digital world while ensuring their well-being is prioritized.

CHAPTER 13

Tools of the Trade

Recommended Software

A re there specific parental control tools or software that you recommend for monitoring and managing a child's online activities?

Certainly! There are several parental control tools and software available that offer a range of features for monitoring and managing a child's online activities. Here are some popular options:

1. **Qustodio**: Qustodio is a comprehensive parental control software that offers features such as website filtering, time limits, social media monitoring, app controls, and location tracking. It supports multiple devices and platforms, including Windows, macOS, Android, and iOS.

2. **Norton Family**: Norton Family provides a wide range of parental control features, including website blocking, time supervision, search monitoring, location tracking, and social network supervision. It supports Windows, macOS, Android, and iOS devices.

3. **Kaspersky Safe Kids**: Kaspersky Safe Kids offers tools for managing screen time, blocking inappropriate content, monitoring social media activity, and tracking the location of your child's device. It works on Windows, macOS, Android, and iOS platforms.

4. **Family Link (by Google)**: Family Link is a free parental control app from Google that allows you to manage your child's device usage, set screen time limits, approve or block apps, track their location, and remotely lock their device. It works on Android and iOS devices.

5. **Net Nanny**: Net Nanny offers features such as web filtering, app blocking, time management, and profanity masking to help parents protect their children from inappropriate content online. It supports Windows, macOS, Android, and iOS platforms.

6. **Screen Time (for iOS)**: Screen Time is a built-in feature on iOS devices that allows parents to set time limits for specific apps or categories of apps, monitor device usage, and restrict access to certain features or content. It can be managed from the parent's iOS device.

7. **OpenDNS FamilyShield**: OpenDNS FamilyShield is a free DNS-based filtering service that blocks access to inappropriate websites at the network level. It can be configured on routers to provide blanket protection for all devices connected to the home network.

These are just a few examples of parental control tools and software available, and the best choice depends on your specific needs and preferences. It's essential to research and evaluate each option to determine which one offers the features and functionality that align with your family's requirements.

Additionally, remember to have open conversations with your child about online safety and the reasons behind implementing parental controls.

CHAPTER 14

Teach Them Early

<u>What advice do you have for teaching children about responsible and safe online behavior, including the importance of not sharing personal information?</u>

Teaching children about responsible and safe online behavior is crucial for helping them navigate the digital world securely. Here are some tips for parents:

1. **Start Early**: Introduce the concept of online safety as soon as your child begins using digital devices. Even young children can understand basic concepts like not talking to strangers online.

2. **Lead by Example**: Model responsible online behavior yourself. Show your children how to protect their privacy, verify information online, and interact respectfully with others.

3. **Establish Clear Rules**: Set clear guidelines for your children's online activities, including what websites they can visit, how much time they can spend online, and what information they should never share online.

4. **Teach Privacy Protection**: Explain the importance of safeguarding personal information such as full name, address, phone number, school name, and photos. Emphasize that this information should not be shared with strangers online.

5. **Use Teachable Moments**: Take advantage of real-life examples or news stories to illustrate the potential risks of sharing personal information online. Discuss how certain actions can have consequences and how to make safe choices online.

6. **Encourage Critical Thinking**: Teach your children to think critically about the information they encounter online. Help them develop the skills to evaluate the credibility and reliability of websites, news articles, and online sources.

7. **Discuss Online Etiquette**: Teach your children about appropriate online behavior, including being respectful to others, avoiding cyberbullying, and thinking twice before posting or sharing anything online.

8. **Promote Open Communication**: Create a supportive environment where your children feel comfortable coming to you with questions or concerns about their online experiences. Encourage them to talk to you if they encounter anything that makes them feel uncomfortable or unsafe online.

9. **Monitor Their Online Activities**: Stay involved in your children's online lives by monitoring their internet usage, reviewing their social media accounts, and periodically checking their browsing history. This helps you stay informed about their online behavior and intervene if necessary.

10. **Stay Informed and Updated**: Keep yourself informed about the latest trends and threats in online safety.

Regularly update your knowledge and discuss new challenges or risks with your children as they arise.

By following these tips and actively engaging with your children about online safety, you can help them develop responsible and safe online habits that will serve them well throughout their lives.

How can parents educate their children about the risks of engaging with strangers online and what steps can be taken to ensure a child's online social circle is safe?

Educating children about the risks of engaging with strangers online is crucial for their safety in the digital world. Here are some steps parents can take to teach their children about this important topic and ensure their online social circle is safe:

1. **Start Early and Have Open Conversations**: Begin talking to your children about online safety from a young age. Use age-appropriate language and examples to explain the concept of strangers and the potential risks of interacting with them online. Encourage your children to ask questions and share their concerns openly.

2. **Teach the Difference Between Friends and Strangers**: Help your children understand the difference between friends and strangers online. Explain that while it's okay to make new friends in safe environments, they should be cautious when communicating with people they don't know online.

3. **Set Clear Boundaries and Guidelines**: Establish clear rules and boundaries for your children's online interactions. Teach them to never share personal information such as their full name, address, phone number, school name, or photos with strangers online. Emphasize the importance of privacy and

safety.

4. **Use Role-Playing and Scenarios**: Role-play different scenarios with your children to help them practice how to respond to requests or messages from strangers online. Teach them to trust their instincts and to immediately report any uncomfortable or suspicious interactions to a trusted adult.

5. **Model Safe Online Behavior**: Set a positive example by demonstrating safe online behavior yourself. Show your children how to interact respectfully with others online, protect their personal information, and verify the identity of people they communicate with.

6. **Monitor Online Activity**: Keep an eye on your children's online activity and social media accounts. Review their friends list and followers to ensure they're only connecting with people they know in real life. Encourage your children to regularly review and update their privacy settings to control who can see their posts and information.

7. **Encourage Safe Communication Channels**: Teach your children to use safe communication channels when interacting with others online. Encourage them to use privacy features such as private messaging or direct messaging rather than public posts or comments.

8. **Establish Trusted Online Communities**: Help your children identify and participate in trusted online communities or platforms that prioritize safety and moderation. Look for platforms with age-appropriate content and robust moderation policies to minimize the risk of encountering strangers or inappropriate content.

9. **Empower Your Children to Say No**: Teach your

children that it's okay to say no to requests or messages from strangers online, even if they feel pressured or uncomfortable. Encourage them to trust their instincts and to seek help from a trusted adult if they're unsure about a situation.

10. **Create a Supportive Environment**: Foster a supportive and non-judgmental environment where your children feel comfortable coming to you with any concerns or questions about their online interactions. Reassure them that you're there to support and guide them in navigating the digital world safely.

By taking these proactive steps and engaging in ongoing conversations about online safety, parents can help empower their children to make safe and responsible choices when interacting with strangers online and ensure their online social circle is safe and supportive.

CHAPTER 15

Issues on the Horizon

<u>Are there any emerging technologies or trends that parents should be particularly aware of in terms of their impact on children's online safety?</u>

Yes, several emerging technologies and trends have significant implications for children's online safety. Parents should be aware of these developments to better protect their children in the digital world. Some notable trends and technologies include:

1. **Artificial Intelligence (AI):**
   - AI-powered algorithms are increasingly being used by social media platforms and online services to personalize content and recommendations.
   - Parents should be aware of how AI algorithms may influence their children's online experiences, including exposure to inappropriate content, targeted advertising, and potential privacy implications.
1. **Internet of Things (IoT) Devices:**
   - IoT devices, such as smart toys, wearables, and home

automation systems, are becoming more prevalent in children's lives.

- Parents should understand the privacy and security risks associated with IoT devices, including data collection practices, vulnerabilities to hacking, and potential risks to children's safety and privacy.

2. **Virtual Reality (VR) and Augmented Reality (AR):**

- VR and AR technologies offer immersive experiences and interactive content that can be appealing to children.
- Parents should monitor their children's use of VR and AR devices and apps, considering potential risks such as exposure to violent or inappropriate content, motion sickness, and privacy concerns.

3. **Online Gaming and Esports:**

- Online gaming and esports continue to grow in popularity among children and teens, with platforms like Twitch and YouTube Gaming attracting millions of viewers.
- Parents should be aware of potential risks associated with online gaming, including exposure to inappropriate content, cyberbullying, online predators, and excessive screen time.

4. **Cryptocurrency and Blockchain:**

- Cryptocurrency and blockchain technologies are increasingly being used in online transactions and digital platforms.
- Parents should educate their children about the risks and challenges of cryptocurrency, including scams, fraud, and illegal activities such as ransomware attacks and money laundering.

5. **Deepfakes and Misinformation:**

- Deepfake technology allows for the creation of highly realistic but fake audio, video, and images, which can be used to spread misinformation and deceive users.
- Parents should teach their children critical thinking skills to evaluate the authenticity of online content and be cautious of sharing or believing information without verification.

Biometric Data and Facial Recognition:

- Biometric data, including facial recognition technology, is increasingly being used for identity verification and authentication in online services and apps.
- Parents should be mindful of the privacy implications of biometric data collection and ensure that their children understand how their biometric information may be used and protected online.

By staying informed about these emerging technologies and trends, parents can better navigate the evolving landscape of children's online safety and take proactive measures to protect their children from potential risks and harms. Additionally, fostering open communication and digital literacy skills can empower children to make safe and responsible choices in the digital world.

CHAPTER 16

Staying Ahead of the Threat

Staying ahead of digital threats in today's interconnected world demands a robust and thorough approach, including education, setting boundaries, implementing security protocols, and maintaining vigilance. Education serves as the cornerstone of cybersecurity. By staying informed about the latest cyber threats, individuals and families can equip themselves with the knowledge needed to recognize and mitigate potential risks. This involves understanding common online scams, practicing good password hygiene, and being aware of the dangers posed by malicious software and phishing attempts.

Boundaries play a crucial role in safeguarding against digital threats, particularly within the family environment. Establishing clear guidelines for internet usage helps to promote responsible online behavior and protect against exposure to harmful content. By setting limits on screen time, specifying which websites are permissible, and delineating rules for sharing personal information online, families can create a safer online environment for all members.

Security protocols are essential for fortifying digital defenses and safeguarding sensitive information. Implementing robust security measures, such as using strong, unique passwords for each online account, enabling two-factor authentication, and regularly updating software and antivirus programs, helps to mitigate the risk of unauthorized access and data breaches.

By extending these protocols to all devices used by family members, including computers, smartphones, and tablets, households can bolster their collective cybersecurity posture.

Vigilance is vital in the ongoing battle against cyber threats. Regularly monitoring online activities, especially those of children and adolescents, enables parents to detect any signs of potential risks or suspicious behavior. Encouraging open communication within the family fosters a supportive environment in which individuals feel comfortable reporting concerns and seeking guidance. By remaining alert to emerging threats and actively addressing any security issues as they arise, families can stay one step ahead of cyber adversaries and minimize the likelihood of falling victim to online threats.

Staying ahead of digital threats requires a proactive and multifaceted approach that incorporates education, setting boundaries, implementing security protocols, and maintaining vigilance. By empowering themselves with knowledge, establishing clear guidelines for online behavior, fortifying their digital defenses, and remaining vigilant in monitoring online activities, families can mitigate the risks posed by cyber threats and create a safer online environment for all members.

---

[1] https://www.missingkids.org/netsmartz/topics/sextortion

www.ingramcontent.com/pod-product-compliance
Lightning Source LLC
Chambersburg PA
CBHW050322230526
45471CB00005B/2308